GOING
Gluten-Free

GOING
Gluten-Free

Breads & Baked Goods With

MARY BROWN

TATE PUBLISHING & *Enterprises*

Published by Tate Publishing & Enterprises, LLC
127 E. Trade Center Terrace | Mustang, Oklahoma 73064 USA
1.888.361.9473 | www.tatepublishing.com

Tate Publishing is committed to excellence in the publishing industry. The company reflects the philosophy established by the founders, based on Psalm 68:11,
"The Lord gave the word and great was the company of those who published it."

Book design copyright © 2009 by Tate Publishing, LLC. All rights reserved.
Cover design by Kandi Evans
Interior design by Stephanie Woloszyn

Published in the United States of America

ISBN: 978-1-60799-804-4
1. Cooking / Health & Healing / General   2. Cooking / General
09.08.10

Dedication

I give thanks for my family, extended family, and friends who have always offered their genuine love and encouragement.

Table of Contents

INTRODUCTION

Living with celiac disease has, undoubtedly, changed your life. Your doctor has told you that celiac disease is an autoimmune disease caused by the body's allergic response to gluten. Gluten is a protein component of wheat, rye, barley, and oats and provides elasticity and cohesiveness to baked products. If someone is allergic to gluten and consumes it, the body's immune system attacks its own tissue and causes disease. In an autoimmune disease, the body attacks itself upon the introduction of a foreign, "toxic" element. In celiac disease, gluten is the "toxic" element, and the small intestine is affected first. The villi are small fingerlike projections in your small intestine and normally absorb nutrients. However, for those allergic to gluten, the body responds by flattening the villi. Your body is therefore unable to absorb nutrients which can result in all sorts of intestinal distress, fatigue, anemia, bone loss, unhealthy weight loss, and in the most serious of cases, certain digestive cancers. Perhaps you belong to the subset of celiacs who are diagnosed with dermatitis herpetiformis. For this group of celiacs, the body also responds negatively to gluten and causes this highly uncomfortable skin condition affecting large areas of the body.

The term "celiac" has Greek and Latin roots, simply referring to the abdominal cavity. Today, those with celiac disease often refer to themselves as "celiacs."

Currently, for those with celiac disease, strictly adhering to the gluten-free diet is the only way to manage the disease. The body will almost always heal itself over time provided that gluten is totally eliminated from the diet. Cheating or "having just a little" will compromise your health. As a celiac, do your best to maintain a positive attitude.

Because most social gatherings involve food, they will also require planning and creativity on your part. Your family and closest friends will help in these situations. There will be occasions, however, when it will be easier to bring your own food or to eat a snack either before you go to the event or after you get home. It is perhaps best to eat something prior to the event to avoid temptation of cheating and irritability due to hunger.

Traveling and eating out pose numerous obstacles as well. You need to pack lots of gluten-free essentials and snacks when away from home. Fortunately, more and more restaurant managers today are aware of gluten-free issues and can help you make wise decisions. However, often you will have to choose very plain entrees to safeguard your health.

If you are just entering the gluten-free arena, you may be worried about finding good tasting food that is free of wheat, rye, barley, and oats. The cost of specialty foods at the grocery store is very often more expensive than "regular" food, and initially there is the overwhelming concern for learning how to make your own gluten-free breads and baked goods. In addition, many gluten-free commercial foods simply don't taste good.

My family, extended family, and friends have given me high praise for the quality of the recipes in this book. They are primarily recipes for breads and baked goods that you really miss when you are first diagnosed with celiac disease. Even if you have been on the gluten-free diet for many years, you will enjoy these recipes.

My family gave me gentle honesty in my earlier attempts but always offered encouragement. After multitudinous experimentation, I know that these recipes work, and the products taste good! You can confidently take them with you as you travel, and you can take them with you to all the parties and potlucks that routinely come along on life's journey.

My book is not a medical book or a substitute for a physician's advice, but it does give you the basic recipes that will help you live your life again. It may take a little practice to get comfortable with the baking process, but there is hope ahead of you. You will be so pleased with the results! You can do it! Let's get started!

Flour Mix

The flour mix is crucial! Mix the following together and use as flour in the recipes. You will want to bookmark this page.

3 c white rice flour *(Personal preference is Kinnikinnick®.)*
1 c tapioca starch *(This is also called tapioca flour.)*
1/2 c potato starch *(Not potato flour)*

Specialty Ingredients to Buy
(Preferences are noted.)

White rice flour *(Kinnikinnick® is preferred.)*
Brown rice flour
Corn flour
Tapioca starch *(This is also called tapioca flour.)*
Potato Starch *(Not potato flour)*
Sorghum flour
Sweet rice flour *(You only need to buy this if you prefer it over sorghum flour.)*
Xanthan gum *(Purchase both Bob's Red Mill® and Ener G® brands.)*

Common Ingredients to Have on Hand

(Gluten-free examples are noted.)

Apple cider vinegar *(Heinz®)*

Baking powder *(Calumet®)*

Baking soda *(Arm and Hammer®)*

Chocolate chips *(Nestle®)*

Cocoa *(Nestle®; Hershey®)*

Cornmeal *(Quaker®)*

Cornstarch *(Argo®)*

Large eggs

Nonstick cooking spray *(Pam® original or Pam® olive oil)*

Shortening *(Crisco®–regular and butter flavored)*

Oils *(Bertolli extra light olive oil distributed by ©Unilever; Mazola® corn oil)*

Sugar *(C & H®)*

Confectioners powdered sugar *(C & H®)*

Brown sugar *(Golden Brown C & H®)*

Salt

Unflavored gelatin *(Knox®)*

Vanilla *(McCormick®)*

Highly active yeast *(Fleischmann's® RapidRise™)*

Substitutions

Often, it seems that after a diagnosis of celiac disease, other sensitivities/allergies surface. For the best taste and texture, follow the recipes in this book "as is." However, substitutions for common ingredients are available in health food stores or online and include the following:

- Egg replacer for eggs *(Ener G®; Orgran®)* These have citric acid derived from corn.

- Tapioca starch or potato starch for cornstarch

- Corn-free baking powder *(Kinnikinnick®)*

- Corn-free flavorings from McCormick® *(Call 1–800–632–5847 for the current list or e-mail McCormick via the mccormick.com website.)*

- Dairy-free milk substitute *(DariFree™ from Vance's™ Foods)* DariFree™ has crystalline fructose from corn.

- Soy-free vegetable shortening *(Spectrum Naturals®)*

- Soy-free chocolate chips *(Enjoy Life®)*

- Sweet rice flour for sorghum flour

- Sugar substitutes *(Follow the instructions of a physician or registered dietitian when choosing a sugar substitute.)*

Sorghum flour is possibly related to corn; therefore, check with a physician or registered dietitian to see if it is safe for you.

When in doubt with any ingredients, seek the advice of a physician or registered dietitian.

Helpful Websites

These are particularly helpful if you have multiple allergies.

www.bobsredmill.com

www.ener-g.com

www.glutenfree.com

www.glutensmart.com

www.kinnikinnick.com

What You Must Accept

Gluten-free products will never taste *exactly* the same as their wheat-based counterparts.

What You Don't Have to Accept

You never have to accept poor taste and poor quality.

Kitchen Equipment and Gadgets to Help Make Your Life Easier

Bread maker–The Panasonic® bread maker is very durable.

Kitchen-Aid® heavy duty stand mixer

8–1/2 x 4–1/2 loaf pans

6–1/4 x 3–1/2 pans

8 x 8 square pan

9 x 9 square pan

Cookie sheets

15 x 10 baking sheet

12-inch or 14-inch nonstick pizza pan

9-inch round cake pan

9-inch pie pan

Muffin pan for 12

Cooling racks

Egg separator

Thermometer capable of measuring below 100°F

Turner or Slotted turner

Many spatulas, accurate measuring cups and measuring spoons

Optional: Silicone pans and bakeware work; gluten-free products release well.

TIPS

Carefully read through the following tips and refer to them often!

- *Mix* the dry ingredients by shaking them in a container with a lid.

- Vegetable oil, butter, stick margarine, or tub margarine may be used in yeast bread recipes. Call the margarine manufacturer to be sure it is gluten-free.

- *Oil* amount may be reduced to half amount in yeast bread recipes, but no lower. Otherwise, the bread will be too sticky.

- *Oil reduction* is not recommended if you are using egg substitutes.

- *Tub margarine* may be used in yeast bread recipes, but use those with a higher vegetable oil content for better taste. Call the manufacturer to be sure the margarine is gluten-free.

- *Gelatin:* This provides moisture to the bread. Omit if your dietary needs require this.

- *Apple cider vinegar:* This helps preserve the bread and adds moisture.

- *To get the water to the desired temperature* when you are not using a bread machine, fill your measuring cup with very hot water from the tap, pour the water into a microwaveable mug, and heat on high for five seconds. Test the temperature with a thermometer and heat in small increments if needed.

- *Gluten-free ingredients work better at room temperature;* therefore you will notice the recipes call for warming the eggs, water, and/or milk.

- *How to foam yeast:*
  - Warm the mixing bowl by running hot water on the outer surface. Wipe dry.
  - Place the yeast in the bowl.
  - Gently pour the sugar water *(warmed to 110°- 115°)* on top of the yeast.
  - Allow the mixture to rest for six minutes.

- *How to separate eggs:*
  - Take two cereal-size bowls and rest the egg separator on one.
  - Crack the egg into the separator and allow the egg white to flow through the separator.
  - Place the yolk into the other bowl.
  - If the white is still clinging to the yolk, gently slip the yolk with remaining white back into the separator and gently shake to try to remove the remaining white.
  - Pour the egg white into the bread batter, using a spatula to get all the white. Never separate the eggs directly into the batter because sometimes the yolk breaks, and then you have too much yolk for the bread.
  - Repeat these steps if you need two whites.

- *Egg yolk measurements:* **Many recipes in this book call for partial yolks measured in teaspoons. Simply separate the egg, break the yolk, and measure with a teaspoon.**

- *How to proof (Let the dough rise):*
  - Place two large bowls or pans on top of a preheated oven near the vent.
  - Place the pan with the dough between the bowls.
  - Place a baking sheet on top of the setup, allowing room for the dough to rise.
  - Finally, cover everything with a towel and allow the dough to rest for one hour.

- *When to use Ener G® xanthan gum and no sorghum flour:*
  - Cakes
  - Brownies
  - Pancakes/waffles
  - Cornbread
  - Banana bread

- *When to use Bob's Red Mill® xanthan gum and sorghum flour:*
  - Breads
  - Rolls
  - Cookies
  - Bars

- *Pan size matters!:* Use the pan size recommended in the recipes for the best turnout. Beware of incorrect pan measurements even when printed by the manufacturer. Measure the pan yourself.

- *Bread notes:* Dry milk and regular milk (all kinds—2%, 1%, and skim) can cause yeast bread and roll recipes to fall; therefore, don't use milk in the yeast bread recipes. Gluten-free bread is more like a thick batter bread. You don't knead the bread because the consistency is so different. It would be impossible to do so.

- *Baking times:* Since oven temperatures can vary, be watchful of times with your oven.

- *Using a bread machine:* For the best quality, it is well worth it to spend ten extra minutes (even just five minutes) beating the ingredients together before placing them into the bread machine. The bread results are greatly improved if you do this! The bread machine's paddle needs this help with gluten-free flours. The Panasonic® bread model has been strong and durable over the years, but perhaps you have a model that works fine without premixing; experiment a little with your machine.

- *Cleanup:* Gluten-free bread batter dries rather quickly on the mixing bowl; therefore immediate cleanup is recommended. Just fill the bowl with warm water right away, and then wipe and wash.

- Wrap the baked breads and cakes with plastic wrap and store them in a plastic bag. Refrigerate or freeze these items after two days.

- Gluten-free bread slices may be microwaved or toasted. Gluten-free cake slices may be microwaved.

- Gluten-free items freeze well.

- Store brown rice flour and sorghum flour in the refrigerator or freezer.

- *Conversion notes for a few recipes:*
  - 1/8 cup = 2 tablespoons *(2T)*
  - 3/8 cup = 1/4 cup + 2T
  - 5/8 cup = 1/2 cup + 2T
  - 3/8 t = 1/4 t + 1/8 t *(t denotes teaspoon)*
  - 5/8 t = 1/2 t + 1/8 t

- *If something goes wrong, try again!*
  - Check the measurements.
  - Check the ingredients.
  - Check the yeast activity if you are making yeast bread. Make sure that the yeast and water foamed. Buy new yeast.

- The accuracy of measuring cups can vary. Therefore, depending on your personal preferences for texture, you may wish to add or subtract one to two tablespoons of the flour mix in the bread recipes.

INSTRUCTIONS FOR THE BREAD MACHINE

Follow these instructions for all of the bread machine recipes. It would be very helpful to bookmark this page.

First, take the yeast out of the refrigerator. Bring the eggs to room temperature by placing them in warm water. As the eggs are warming, proceed to get all the other ingredients ready.

Mix the dry ingredients except for the yeast, shake in a container with a lid, and set aside.

Place the room-temperature measured water in the mixing bowl.

Separate the eggs *(see "Tips")* and add the required amount to the water. Add the remaining liquid ingredients. Gradually blend in the dry ingredients, scraping the bowl.

Beat for 10 minutes. *(See "Tips.")*

Use a spatula to pour/scrape the batter into the bread pan. Close the lid, add the yeast in the dispenser, and press "start" for the bake mode. The bread will be done in 4 hours using the Panasonic® bread maker model. If the yeast is mixed in with the dry ingredients rather than in the dispenser, the loaf will be flattened on top. Therefore, be sure to place the yeast in the dispenser.

Cleanup: Immediate cleanup of the mixing bowl is recommended. *(See "Tips.")*

Cool the bread on its side on a cooling rack. Cool completely before slicing.

Note: The bread will not rise as much as when using gluten-containing flours. Expect this, but know that the taste is great!

Egg Substitute Instructions for the Bread Machine

For 2 eggs, use 2T + 2t Ener G® Egg Replacer™. Mix with the dry ingredients and add an additional 1/3 cup room-temperature water. Even if the recipe calls for 2 egg whites, go ahead and use the amount of Egg Replacer™ just indicated.

For 3 eggs or 3 egg whites, use 4T Ener G® Egg Replacer™. Mix with the dry ingredients and add an additional 1/2 cup room-temperature water.

INSTRUCTIONS FOR BREAD IN THE OVEN

Follow Option A or Option B for all the yeast bread and dinner roll recipes for the oven. It would be helpful to bookmark this page as well.

Option A

Preheat the oven to 375°.

Take the yeast out of the refrigerator. Bring the eggs to room temperature by placing them in warm water. As the eggs are warming, proceed to get all the other ingredients ready.

Mix the dry ingredients except for the yeast, shake in a container with a lid, and set aside.

Spray the pan with vegetable no-stick cooking spray.

Warm the mixing bowl by running hot water on the outside. Wipe dry.

Foam the yeast and sugar water in the mixing bowl for 6 minutes. Water should be about 114°. *(See "Tips" for how to do this.)*

While the yeast is foaming, separate the eggs. *(See "Tips.")*

After 6 minutes, add the required amount of eggs, oil, and vinegar to the foaming mixture. Mix slightly.

Carefully add the dry ingredients and beat 10 minutes.

Use a spatula to place the dough into the pan. Cover and let rise 1 hour on top of the preheated stove. *(See "Tips" for proofing.)*

For the 8–1/2 x 4–1/2 pan, bake for 20 minutes uncovered and then 12 more minutes loosely covered with aluminum foil.

For the 9–1/2 x 5–1/2 pan, bake for 20 minutes uncovered and then 17 more minutes loosely covered with aluminum foil.

Release the bread immediately and cool the loaf on its side on a cooling rack. You may need to use a plastic knife or toothpick to help release the bread. Cool completely before slicing.

The advantage of using Option A is seeing the yeast foam. You know early in the process that your recipe will work.

Option B

Preheat the oven to 375°.

Take the yeast out of the refrigerator. Bring the eggs to room temperature by placing them in warm water. As the eggs are warming, proceed to get all the other ingredients ready.

Include the yeast in the dry ingredients, shake in a container with a lid, and set aside.

Skip the foaming step.

Spray the pan with vegetable no-stick cooking spray.

Separate the eggs. *(See "Tips.")*

Warm the mixing bowl by running hot water on the outside. Wipe dry.

Put the required amount of eggs, oil, and vinegar into the mixing bowl and mix slightly.

Add the dry ingredients and then the water warmed to 120°-130° (125° works).

Beat 10 minutes and continue as outlined in Option A.

Egg Substitute Instructions for Bread in the Oven

For 2 eggs, use 2T + 2t Ener G® Egg Replacer™. Mix with the dry ingredients and add an additional 1/3 cup room-temperature water when you would have added the eggs. Even if the recipe calls for 2 egg whites, go ahead and use the amount of Egg Replacer™ just indicated.

For 3 eggs or 3 egg whites, use 4T Ener G® Egg Replacer™. Mix with the dry ingredients and add an additional 1/2 cup room-temperature water when you would have added the eggs.

YEAST BREADS

White Bread in the Bread Machine

See Instructions for the Bread Machine.
Ingredients for a smaller loaf: (This size is recommended for the best taste.)

Dry:

2c + 2T flour mix
2t sorghum flour
2t cornstarch
2T + 2–1/2 t granulated sugar
2t Bob's Red Mill® xanthan gum
1t salt
1/4 t unflavored gelatin
1t highly active yeast *(Fleischmann's®*
  RapidRise™)

Liquid:

1c water
2 large egg whites
1t egg yolk *(omit if desired or allergic)*
1/4 c corn oil
1t apple cider vinegar

Variation: Instead of the amount of granulated sugar listed above, use 2T + 1/2 t brown sugar and 2t granulated sugar. The brown sugar needn't be packed.

Measurements for a larger loaf:

Dry:

3c + 3T flour mix
1T sorghum flour
1T cornstarch
4T + 1t granulated sugar
1T Bob's Red Mill® xanthan gum
1-1/2 t salt
3/8 t unflavored gelatin *(1/4 t + 1/8 t)*
1-1/2 t highly active yeast *(Fleischmann's®
    RapidRise™)*

Liquid:

1-1/2 c water
3 large egg whites
1-1/2 t egg yolk *(omit if desired or allergic)*
3/8 c corn oil *(1/4 c + 2T)*
1-1/2 t apple cider vinegar

Variation: Instead of the amount of granulated sugar listed above, use 3T + 1t brown sugar and 1T granulated sugar. The brown sugar needn't be packed.

White Bread in the Oven

See Instructions for Bread in the Oven.

Ingredients for a smaller loaf: (This size is recommended for the best taste.) 8–1/2 x 4–1/2 pan

Dry:

- 2c + 2T flour mix
- 2t sorghum flour
- 2t cornstarch
- 2T + 1/2 t granulated sugar OR unpacked brown sugar
- 2t Bob's Red Mill® xanthan gum
- 1t salt
- 1/4 t unflavored gelatin
- 1t highly active yeast (*Fleischmann's® RapidRise™*)

Liquid:

- 1c water with 2t additional granulated sugar dissolved
- 2 large egg whites
- 1t egg yolk *(omit if desired or allergic)*
- 1/4 c corn oil
- 1t apple cider vinegar

Measurements for a larger loaf: 9–1/2 x 5–1/2 pan

Dry:

- 3c + 3T flour mix
- 1T sorghum flour
- 1T cornstarch
- 3T + 1t granulated sugar OR unpacked brown sugar
- 1T Bob's Red Mill® xanthan gum
- 1–1/2 t salt
- 3/8 t unflavored gelatin (*1/4 t + 1/8 t*)
- 1–1/2 t highly active yeast (*Fleischmann's® RapidRise™*)

Liquid:

- 1–1/2 c water with 1T additional granulated sugar dissolved
- 3 large egg whites
- 1–1/2 t egg yolk *(omit if desired or allergic)*
- 3/8 c corn oil (*1/4 c + 2T*)
- 1–1/2 t apple cider vinegar

Notes

Use Option A or Option B baking instructions for either loaf, noting the time differences for the size loaf you are baking.

If you are baking according to Option B, you don't need to dissolve the sugar in the water. Put the sugar you would have dissolved into the dry ingredients.

White Rice and Brown Rice Bread in the Bread Machine

See Instructions for the Bread Machine.
Ingredients for a smaller loaf: (This size is recommended for the best taste.)

Dry:

- 1–1/2 c flour mix
- 2/3 c brown rice flour
- 2t sorghum flour
- 2t cornstarch
- 2T + 1/2 t brown sugar *(Unpacked is okay.)*
- 2t granulated sugar
- 2t Bob's Red Mill® xanthan gum
- 1t salt
- 1/4 t unflavored gelatin
- 1–1/8 t highly active yeast *(Fleischmann's® RapidRise™)*

Liquid:

- 1c water
- 2 large egg whites
- 1t egg yolk *(omit if desired or allergic)*
- 1/4 c corn oil
- 1t apple cider vinegar

Measurements for a larger loaf:

Dry:

- 2–1/4 c flour mix
- 1c brown rice flour
- 1T sorghum flour
- 1T cornstarch
- 3T + 1t brown sugar *(Unpacked is okay.)*
- 1T granulated sugar
- 1T Bob's Red Mill® xanthan gum
- 1–1/2 t salt
- 3/8 t unflavored gelatin *(1/4 t + 1/8 t)*
- 1–1/2 t highly active yeast *(Fleischmann's® RapidRise™)*

Liquid:

- 1–1/2 c water
- 3 large egg whites
- 1–1/2 t egg yolk *(omit if desired or allergic)*
- 3/8 c corn oil *(1/4 c + 2T)*
- 1–1/2 t apple cider vinegar

White Rice and Brown Rice Bread in the Oven

See Instructions for Bread in the Oven.

Ingredients for a smaller loaf: (This size is recommended for the best taste.) 8–1/2 x 4–1/2 pan

Dry:

1–1/2 c flour mix
2/3 c brown rice flour
2t sorghum flour
2t cornstarch
2T + 1/2 t brown sugar *(Unpacked is okay.)*
2t Bob's Red Mill® xanthan gum
1t salt
1/4 t unflavored gelatin
1–1/8 t highly active yeast *(Fleischmann's® RapidRise™)*

Liquid:

1c water with 2t additional granulated sugar dissolved
2 large egg whites
1t egg yolk *(omit if desired or allergic)*
1/4 c corn oil
1t apple cider vinegar

Measurements for a larger loaf: 9–1/2 x 5–1/2 pan

Dry:

2–1/4 c flour mix
1c brown rice flour
1T sorghum flour
1T cornstarch
3T + 1t brown sugar *(Unpacked is okay.)*
1T Bob's Red Mill® xanthan gum
1–1/2 t salt
3/8 t unflavored gelatin *(1/4 t + 1/8 t)*
1–1/2t highly active yeast *(Fleischmann's® RapidRise™)*

Liquid:

1–1/2 c water with 1T additional granulated sugar dissolved
3 large egg whites
1–1/2 t egg yolk *(omit if desired or allergic)*
3/8 c corn oil *(1/4 c + 2T)*
1–1/2 t apple cider vinegar

Notes

Use Option A or Option B baking instructions for either loaf, noting the time differences for the size loaf you are baking.

If you are baking according to Option B, you don't need to dissolve the sugar in the water. Put the sugar you would have dissolved into the dry ingredients.

Imitation Rye Bread in the Bread Machine

See Instructions for the Bread Machine.
Ingredients for a smaller loaf: (This size is recommended for the best taste.)

Dry:

1–1/2 c flour mix
2/3 c brown rice flour
2t sorghum flour
2t cornstarch
2T + 1/2 t brown sugar *(Unpacked is okay.)*
2t granulated sugar
2t Bob's Red Mill® xanthan gum
1t salt
1/4 t unflavored gelatin
1t caraway seeds
1–1/8 t highly active yeast *(Fleischmann's®
RapidRise™)*

Liquid:

1c water
2 large egg whites
1t egg yolk *(omit if desired or allergic)*
1/4 c corn oil
1t apple cider vinegar

Measurements for a larger loaf:

Dry:

- 2–1/4 c flour mix
- 1c brown rice flour
- 1T sorghum flour
- 1T cornstarch
- 3T + 1t brown sugar *(Unpacked is okay.)*
- 1T granulated sugar
- 1T Bob's Red Mill® xanthan gum
- 1–1/2 t salt
- 3/8 t unflavored gelatin *(1/4 t + 1/8 t)*
- 1–1/2 t caraway seeds
- 1–3/4 t highly active yeast *(Fleischmann's® RapidRise™)*

Liquid:

- 1–1/2 c water
- 3 large egg whites
- 1–1/2 t egg yolk *(omit if desired or allergic)*
- 3/8 c corn oil *(1/4 c + 2T)*
- 1–1/2 t apple cider vinegar

GOING GLUTEN-FREE

Imitation Rye Bread in the Oven

See Instructions for Bread in the Oven.
Ingredients for a smaller loaf: (This size is recommended for the best taste.) 8–1/2 x 4–1/2 pan

Dry:

1–1/2 c flour mix
2/3 c brown rice flour
2t sorghum flour
2t cornstarch
2T + 1/2 t brown sugar *(Unpacked is okay.)*
2t Bob's Red Mill® xanthan gum
1t salt
1/4 t unflavored gelatin
1t caraway seeds
1–1/8 t highly active yeast *(Fleischmann's® RapidRise™)*

Liquid:

1c water with 2t additional granulated sugar dissolved
2 large egg whites
1t egg yolk *(omit if desired or allergic)*
1/4 c corn oil
1t apple cider vinegar

Measurements for a larger loaf: 9–1/2 x 5–1/2 pan

Dry:

2–1/4 c flour mix
1c brown rice flour
1T sorghum flour
1T cornstarch
3T + 1t brown sugar *(Unpacked is okay.)*
1T Bob's Red Mill® xanthan gum
1–1/2 t salt
3/8 t unflavored gelatin *(1/4 t + 1/8 t)*
1–1/2 t caraway seeds
1–3/4 t highly active yeast *(Fleischmann's® RapidRise™)*

Liquid:

1–1/2 c water with 1T additional granulated sugar dissolved
3 large egg whites
1–1/2 t egg yolk *(omit if desired or allergic)*
3/8 c corn oil *(1/4 c + 2T)*
1–1/2 t apple cider vinegar

Notes

Use Option A or Option B baking instructions for either loaf, noting the time differences for the size loaf you are baking.

If you are baking according to Option B, you don't need to dissolve the sugar in the water. Put the sugar you would have dissolved into the dry ingredients.

Imitation Italian Bread in the Bread Machine

See Instructions for the Bread Machine.

Notice the sugar amount has changed from the white bread recipe. Even if you omit the sugar, the recipe will work!

Ingredients for a smaller loaf: (This size is recommended for the best taste.)

Dry:

- 2c + 2T flour mix
- 2t sorghum flour
- 2t cornstarch
- 2t granulated sugar
- 2t Bob's Red Mill® xanthan gum
- 1t salt
- 1/4 t unflavored gelatin
- 1t highly active yeast *(Fleischmann's® RapidRise™)*

Liquid:

- 1c water
- 2 large egg whites
- 1t egg yolk *(omit if desired or allergic)*
- 1/4 c corn oil
- 1t apple cider vinegar

Measurements for a larger loaf:

Dry:

- 3c + 3T flour mix
- 1T sorghum flour
- 1T cornstarch
- 1T granulated sugar
- 1T Bob's Red Mill® xanthan gum
- 1-1/2 t salt
- 3/8 t unflavored gelatin *(1/4 t + 1/8 t)*
- 1-1/2 t highly active yeast *(Fleischmann's® RapidRise™)*

Liquid:

- 1-1/2 c water
- 3 large egg whites
- 1-1/2 t egg yolk *(omit if desired or allergic)*
- 3/8 c corn oil *(1/4 c + 2T)*
- 1-1/2 t apple cider vinegar

Imitation Italian Bread in the Oven

See Instructions for Bread in the Oven.

Notice the sugar amount has changed from the white bread recipe. Even if you omit the sugar, the recipe will work!

Ingredients for a smaller loaf: (This size is recommended for the best taste.) 8–1/2 x 4–1/2 pan

Dry:

- 2c + 2T flour mix
- 2t sorghum flour
- 2t cornstarch
- 2t Bob's Red Mill® xanthan gum
- 1t salt
- 1/4 t unflavored gelatin
- 1t highly active yeast *(Fleischmann's® RapidRise™)*

Liquid:

- 1c water with 2t granulated sugar dissolved
- 2 large egg whites
- 1t egg yolk *(omit if desired or allergic)*
- 1/4 c corn oil
- 1t apple cider vinegar

Measurements for a larger loaf: 9–1/2 x 5–1/2 pan

Dry:

- 3c + 3T flour mix
- 1T sorghum flour
- 1T cornstarch
- 1T Bob's Red Mill® xanthan gum
- 1–1/2 t salt
- 3/8 t unflavored gelatin *(1/4 t + 1/8 t)*
- 1–1/2 t highly active yeast *(Fleischmann's® RapidRise™)*

Liquid:

- 1–1/2 c water with 1T granulated sugar dissolved
- 3 large egg whites
- 1–1/2 t egg yolk *(omit if desired or allergic)*
- 3/8 c corn oil *(1/4 c + 2T)*
- 1–1/2 t apple cider vinegar

Notes

Use Option A or Option B baking instructions for either loaf, noting the time differences for the size loaf you are baking.

If you are baking according to Option B, you don't need to dissolve the sugar in the water. Put the sugar you would have dissolved into the dry ingredients.

White Sandwich Buns, Hotdog & Hamburger Buns

Follow the recipe for White Bread in the Oven.

Lightly spray a baking sheet with vegetable spray.

Follow Option A or Option B instructions under Instructions for Bread in the Oven except for the baking time.

Once you have the dough ready, spoon the dough onto the baking sheet, and use a spatula to gently shape the buns.

The recipe will make 8 buns.

Proof according to "Tips."

Bake at 375° for 16–18 minutes. Release immediately and cool upside down on a cooling rack.

Hot Dog Bun Issues

These are a little tricky to make with just a baking sheet. The dough is a little sticky, and it does not quite hold its form. The finished product is a little flatter than store bought buns. However, the process is definitely manageable. Bake the buns close together on the baking sheet. Unfortunately, hot dog pans are available on the internet from Cook's Direct which sells only to food distributors and food service operations. However, New England style hotdog bun pans are available from kingarthurflour.com.

Dinner Rolls

These have more egg yolk for flavor. They taste great with butter or your favorite spread. (Of course, the extra egg yolk isn't required, depending on your needs or taste. You may simply follow the White Bread recipe for dinner rolls.) Note that there is no gelatin in this recipe.

Dry:

- 2c + 2T flour mix
- 2t sorghum flour
- 2t cornstarch
- 2T + 1/2 t granulated sugar
- 2t Bob's Red Mill® xanthan gum
- 1t salt
- 1t highly active yeast *(Fleischmann's® RapidRise™)*

Liquid:

- 1c water with 2t additional granulated sugar dissolved
- 1 whole egg + 1 egg white
- 1/4 c corn oil
- 1t apple cider vinegar

Preheat the oven to 375°.

This will make 12 dinner rolls. Lightly spray a muffin pan with vegetable spray.

Follow Option A or Option B instructions under Instructions for Bread in the Oven except for the baking time. If you are following Option B, place all the sugar in the dry ingredients.

Once you have the dough ready, spoon the dough into the muffin pan for 12.

Proof according to "Tips" for an hour, and then bake at 375° for 15–16 minutes.

Let the rolls sit in the pan for 3 minutes, release, and then cool them upside down on a cooling rack.

Variations: For smaller dinner rolls, spoon smaller amounts of the dough into 12 muffin cups and the remaining dough into a mini loaf pan (6–1/4 x 3–1/2) for a larger roll. Proof, and bake the smaller dinner rolls for 15 minutes at 375° and the larger roll for 16 minutes.

Or place half of the dough into a mini loaf pan (6–1/4 x 3–1/2) and spoon the rest into 8 muffin cups. Proof, and bake the rolls for 15–16 minutes at 375° and the loaf for 18 minutes.

Italian Dinner Rolls

Notice the sugar amount has changed from the white bread recipe. Even if you omit the sugar, the recipe will work!

Dry:

- 2c + 2T flour mix
- 2t sorghum flour
- 2t cornstarch
- 2t Bob's Red Mill® xanthan gum
- 1t salt
- 1/4 t unflavored gelatin
- 1t highly active yeast *(Fleischmann's® RapidRise™)*

Liquid:

- 1c water with 2t granulated sugar dissolved
- 2 egg whites
- 1t egg yolk *(omit if desired or allergic)*
- 1/4 c corn oil
- 1t apple cider vinegar

This will make 13 dinner rolls. Use a muffin pan and a mini loaf pan (6–1/4 x 3–1/2) for a large roll.

Preheat the oven to 375°.

Lightly spray a muffin pan and a mini loaf pan (6–1/4 x 3–1/2) with vegetable spray.

Follow Option A or Option B instructions under Instructions for Bread in the Oven except for the baking time. If you are following Option B, place the sugar in the dry ingredients.

Once you have the dough ready, spoon the dough into the muffin pan (for the 12) and the remaining batter into the mini loaf pan.

Proof according to "Tips" for an hour, and then bake at 375° for 16–18 minutes.

Let the rolls sit in the pans for 3 minutes, release, and then cool upside down on a cooling rack.

Pizza Crust

The sugar amount may be omitted, and the recipe still works!

Dry:

- 1c + 1T flour mix
- 1t sorghum flour
- 1t cornstarch
- 1t Bob's Red Mill® xanthan gum
- 1/2 t salt
- 1/8 t unflavored gelatin
- 1/2 t highly active yeast *(Fleischmann's® RapidRise™)*

Liquid:

- 1/2 c water with 1/2 t granulated sugar dissolved
- 1 egg white
- 1/2 t egg yolk *(omit if desired or allergic)*
- 1–1/2 T corn oil
- 1/2 t apple cider vinegar

Preheat the oven to 375°.

Lightly spray a pizza pan with vegetable spray. Sprinkle the pan with sesame seeds if desired.

Follow Option A or Option B instructions under Instructions for Bread in the Oven except for the baking time. If you are following Option B, place the sugar in the dry ingredients.

Once the dough is ready, use a spatula to scrape the dough onto the pizza pan.

Use a turner or slotted turner to spread the dough to roughly 10 inches.

Proof according to "Tips."

Bake at 375° for 20 minutes. Release immediately and cool upside down on a cooling rack. Use right away, or freeze for later use.

Tips

Sesame seeds, garlic salt, and pepper add flavor to the pizza sauce. Put the sauce and toppings on, and broil on low for about 7 minutes. You can also place toppings on the crust before the sauce.

If you are using a frozen crust, thaw it first, toast slices or crisp them in a 400° oven for 3 minutes. Then place the toppings on and broil on low for about 7 minutes.

All-Purpose Flatbread

Use a 15 x 10 baking sheet.
Use this for sandwich bread, dinner bread, toast, stuffing cubes, and pizza crust.

Dry:

2c + 2T flour mix
2t sorghum flour
2t cornstarch
2T + 1/2 t granulated sugar
2t Bob's Red Mill® xanthan gum
1t salt
1/4 t unflavored gelatin
1t highly active yeast (Fleischmann's®
    RapidRise™)

Liquid:

1c water with 2t additional granulated
    sugar dissolved
2 egg whites
1t egg yolk (omit if desired or allergic)
1/4 c corn oil
1t apple cider vinegar

Preheat the oven to 375°.

Lightly spray the baking sheet with vegetable spray. Sprinkle the sheet with sesame seeds if desired.

Follow Option A or Option B instructions under Instructions for Bread in the Oven except for the baking time. If you are following Option B, place all the sugar in the dry ingredients.

Once the dough is ready, use a spatula to scrape the dough onto the baking sheet.

Use a turner or slotted turner to spread the dough to roughly 14 x 9 inches.

Proof according to "Tips."

Bake at 375° for 24 minutes. Release immediately and cool upside down on cooling racks.

Cut pieces to whatever size you want. Use right away, or freeze for later use.

YEAST-FREE BREADS

Yeast-free breads may be flavored with caraway or sesame seeds. Add 1t of either kind to the dry ingredients or simply sprinkle the desired amount in your sandwich or on your toast. Unpacked brown sugar may also be used in place of the granulated sugar. Oil reduction is not recommended in yeast-free recipes.

Basic Yeast-Free Bread

8–1/2 x 4–1/2 pan

Dry:

2–1/4 c flour mix
2t sorghum flour
2T + 2–1/2 t granulated sugar
3t baking powder
1t salt (can be reduced to 3/4 t)
1t Bob's Red Mill® xanthan gum

Liquid:

2–1/2 egg whites (visually approximate or use 16.5 cc for the 1/2 white. Use a child's medicine dispenser to measure.)
1t egg yolk
1c 2% milk
1/4 c corn oil
2t Ener G® Egg Replacer™
1T + 1t water

Preheat the oven to 375°.

Warm the eggs in very warm water.

Shake the dry ingredients, except for the Ener G® Egg Replacer™, in a closed container and then place in the mixing bowl.

Warm the milk for 40 seconds on medium in the microwave.

Separate the eggs. (See "Tips.")

Add the liquid ingredients, except the final 1T + 1t water, to the dry ingredients and blend.

Mix the Ener G® Egg Replacer™ and 1T + 1t water in a separate small bowl or cup and add to the mixture. Beat for 3 minutes.

Pour the batter into the lightly sprayed pan, but don't spread it out or flatten it. Bake at 375° for 20 minutes. Cover loosely with aluminum foil and bake for 20 more minutes. Remove the foil and bake for 5 more minutes (45 minutes in total). Remove the bread immediately from the pan and cool it on its side on a cooling rack. You might need to use a plastic knife or toothpick to help with the release. Cool completely before slicing.

Yeast-Free Pizza Crust or Dinner Rolls

Dry:

- 1–1/8 c flour mix
- 1t sorghum flour
- 1T + 1–1/4 t granulated sugar
- 1–1/2 t baking powder
- 1/4 t salt (1/2 t for dinner rolls)
- 1/2 t Bob's Red Mill® xanthan gum

Liquid:

- 1 egg white + 2t additional egg white
- 1/2 t egg yolk
- 1/2 c 2% milk
- 2T corn oil
- 1t Ener G®EggReplacer™ mixed with
  2t water

Pizza Crust: Follow the mixing and beating instructions for yeast-free bread, and then spread the dough to about 10 inches with a slotted turner on a lightly sprayed pizza pan. Bake at 375° for 18–20 minutes. Release the crust immediately and cool it upside down on a cooling rack.

Dinner Rolls: Follow the mixing and beating instructions for yeast-free bread, and then use a spatula to fill 8 muffins in a lightly sprayed muffin pan. Bake at 375° for 16–18 minutes. Let the rolls sit in the pans for 3 minutes, release, and then cool them upside down on a cooling rack.

Yeast-Free Buttermilk Bread

8–1/2 x 4–1/2 pan

Dry:

- 2–1/4 c flour mix
- 2t sorghum flour
- 2T + 2–1/2 t granulated sugar
- 2t baking powder
- 1/2 t baking soda
- 1/2 t salt
- 4T buttermilk powder *(Saco® brand)*
- 1t Bob's Red Mill® xanthan gum

Liquid:

- 2–1/2 egg whites *(visually approximate or use 16.5 cc for the 1/2 white. Use a child's medicine dispenser to measure.)*
- 1t egg yolk
- 1c water
- 1/4 c corn oil
- 2t EnerG®Egg Replacer™
- 1T +1t water

Preheat the oven to 375°.

Warm the eggs in very warm water.

Shake the dry ingredients including the buttermilk powder in a closed container and then place in the mixing bowl. Don't add the Ener G® Egg Replacer™ yet.

Warm the 1 cup water for 40 seconds on medium in the microwave.

Separate the eggs. (See "Tips.")

Add the liquid ingredients, except the final 1T +1t water, to the dry ingredients and blend.

Mix the Ener G® Egg Replacer™ and 1T +1t water in a separate small bowl or cup and add to the mixture. Beat for 3 minutes.

Pour the batter into the lightly sprayed pan, but don't spread it out or flatten it. Bake at 375° for 20 minutes. Cover loosely with aluminum foil and bake for 20 more minutes. Remove the foil and bake for 5 more minutes (45 minutes in total). Remove the bread immediately from the pan and cool it on its side on a cooling rack. You might need to use a plastic knife or toothpick to help with the release. Cool completely before slicing.

CAKES

After first missing bread, many celiacs then think about all the assorted baked goods that are on the "Do Not Eat" list. However, cake can definitely be a part of a gluten-free diet. These recipes will not disappoint! The white cake is very moist and so good! Just as delightful as the white cake, chocolate cake and cupcakes are easy to take along on picnics or when you need to bring a dessert to share at a gathering. The applesauce egg-free cake is a wonderful treat on a fall day or any day.

White Cake

For the 8–1/2 x 4–1/2 pan

Dry:

- 1–1/8 c flour mix
- 5/8 c granulated sugar (1/2 c + 2T)
- 2t baking powder
- 1/2 t salt
- 1/2 t Ener G® xanthan gum

Liquid:

- 1 egg
- 1/4 c extra light olive oil
- 1/2 t vanilla
- 2–1/4 t lemon juice
- 1/2 c 2% milk warmed on medium for 40 seconds in the microwave

Preheat the oven to 325°.

Warm the egg in very warm water.

Shake the dry ingredients in a container with a lid and set aside.

Beat the egg in the mixing bowl.

Add the oil, vanilla, and lemon juice. Don't beat these.

Add the mixed dry ingredients and then the milk.

Blend these, and then beat for 3 minutes. Pour the batter into a lightly sprayed 8–1/2 x 4–1/2 pan and bake for 42 minutes. The cake is done when a toothpick inserted in the middle comes out clean. Cool completely and remove the cake from the pan for easy slicing. This recipe will also make 12 cupcakes, baked in a muffin pan at 350° for 20 minutes.

Variation: Another combination that works is 1–1/2 c flour mix with 3/4 c granulated sugar. The remaining ingredients and bake time are the same.

For *chocolate chip muffins* with the basic ingredients, use 1/4 c Crisco® shortening in place of the olive oil and add this before the milk. Beat for 3 minutes and then stir in 1/4 c mini chocolate chips. This recipe makes 10 muffins. Bake at 350° for 15–17 minutes.

Tips: First, pour the batter into a pitcher. Then pour the batter into the muffin cups. Paper liners work very well. Remove the cupcakes from the pan and cool completely before peeling away the paper.

For *cinnamon streusel topping*, use a fork to form a crumbly mixture with 2T of the flour mixture, 1T brown sugar, 1T tub margarine, and 1/8 t cinnamon. Sprinkle it on the white cake before baking at 325° for 42 minutes. The mixture will sink into the cake, and it tastes great! If you want the streusel topping to stay on top of the cake, use 1T butter instead of the tub margarine.

White Cake

For the 9–1/2 x 5–1/2 pan or 9-inch round cake pan

Dry:

- 1–3/4 c flour mix
- 1c granulated sugar
- 3 t baking powder (1T)
- 3/4 t salt
- 3/4 t Ener G® xanthan gum

Liquid:

- 1–1/2 eggs *(visually approximate)*
- 3/8 c extra light olive oil *(1/4 c + 2T)*
- 3/4 t vanilla
- 1T + 1/2 t lemon juice
- 3/4 c 2% milk warmed on medium for 40 seconds in the microwave.

Follow the mixing and beating instructions for White Cake for the smaller pan.

For the 9–1/2 x 5–1/2 pan, bake at 325° for 46 minutes.

For the 9-inch round pan, bake at 350° for 37–40 minutes.

The cake is done when a toothpick inserted in the middle comes out clean.

Variation: Another combination that works is 2–1/4 c flour mix with 1–1/4 c granulated sugar. The remaining ingredients and bake time are the same.

Angel Food Cake

Use the 8–1/2 x 4–1/2 pan.

Dry:

- 1–1/2 c flour mix
- 1/2 c + 1/3c granulated sugar
- 2t baking powder
- 1/2 t salt
- 1/2 t Ener G® xanthan gum

Liquid:

- 1–1/2 egg whites *(visually approximate or use 16.5 cc egg white for the 1/2 white. Use a child's medicine dispenser to measure.)*
- 1/3 c extra light olive oil
- 1/2 t almond extract
- 2–1/4 t lemon juice
- 1/2 c 2% milk warmed on medium for 40 seconds in the microwave.

Preheat the oven to 325°.

Warm the eggs in very warm water.

Shake the dry ingredients in a container with a lid and set aside.

Separate the eggs. *(See "Tips.")*

Beat the egg whites in the mixing bowl.

Add the oil, almond extract, and lemon juice. Don't beat these.

Add the mixed dry ingredients and then the milk. Blend these, and then beat for 3 minutes. Pour the batter into a lightly sprayed 8–1/2 x 4–1/2 pan and bake for 43–44 minutes. The cake is done when a toothpick inserted in the middle comes out clean. Cool completely and remove the cake from the pan for easy slicing.

Applesauce Egg-Free Cake

Use an 8 x 8 pan.

Dry:

- 1–2/3 c flour mix
- 1 c brown sugar
- 1 t baking soda
- 1/2 t salt
- 1/2 t Ener G® xanthan gum

Liquid:

- 1/2 c warm water
- 1/3 c corn oil
- 1 t apple cider vinegar
- 1/2 c cinnamon applesauce

Preheat the oven to 350°.

Shake the dry ingredients in a container with a lid and place in a mixing bowl.

Stir in the remaining ingredients.

Place the thick batter into an 8 x 8 pan (very lightly sprayed with vegetable spray) and spread with a spatula. Bake for 30 minutes, and cool the pan on a cooling rack. Frost with vanilla frosting if desired.

Cake Donuts Baked as Muffins

These cake donuts avoid frying!

Ingredients:

1c flour mix

1/4 c granulated sugar

1t baking powder

1/2 t salt

1/4 t apple pie spice

1/2 t Ener G® xanthan gum

1/4 t highly active yeast (Fleischmann's®
RapidRise™)

1/2 egg (visually approximate) beaten

2T Crisco® shortening

1/4 c 2% milk heated to 125°

Preheat the oven to 375°.

Warm the egg in very warm water.

Shake the dry ingredients in a sealed container and set aside.

Beat the 1/2 egg in the mixing bowl and then add the dry ingredients and Crisco® shortening.

Pour the hot milk on top, blend, and beat for 3 minutes.

Spoon the batter into a muffin pan (makes 8). Cover and let rest for 20 minutes on top of the stove.

Bake at 375° for 12 minutes.

Cool in the pan for a minute and then roll the muffin donuts in powdered sugar.

Yeast-Free Cake Donuts Baked as Muffins

Omit the yeast, and increase the baking powder to 1-1/2 t. Follow the mixing instructions above, but there is no need to cover and let the batter rest. Bake at 375° for 10–12 minutes. Cool in the pan for a minute and then roll the muffin donuts in powdered sugar.

Chocolate Cake

For the 8–1/2 x 4–1/2 pan

Dry:

- 1–1/8 c flour mix
- 1/2 c + 1/3 c granulated sugar
- 1/3 c cocoa
- 5/8 t baking soda *(1/2 t + 1/8t)*
- 1/2 t salt
- 1/8 t baking powder
- 1/2 t Ener G® xanthan gum

Liquid:

- 1 egg
- 3/8 c extra light olive oil *(1/4 c + 2T)*
- 1/2 t vanilla
- 5/8 c warm water *(1/2 c + 2T)*

Preheat the oven to 350°.

Warm the egg in very warm water.

Shake the dry ingredients in a container with a lid and set aside.

Beat the egg in the mixing bowl.

Add the oil and vanilla. Don't beat these.

Add the mixed dry ingredients and then the warm water.

Blend these, and then beat for 3 minutes. Pour into a lightly sprayed 8–1/2 x 4–1/2 pan and bake for 40–42 minutes. The cake is done when a toothpick inserted in the middle comes out clean. Cool completely and remove the cake from the pan for easy slicing.

Chocolate Cupcakes

Follow the mixing and beating instructions above. The recipe makes 12 cupcakes. Bake at 350° for 20 minutes. Paper liners work very well. Remove the cupcakes from the pan and cool completely before peeling away the paper.

Tip: First, pour the batter into a pitcher. Then pour the batter into the lined muffin cups.

Chocolate Cake

For the 9–1/2 x 5–1/2 pan or 9-inch round cake pan

Dry:

- 1–3/4 c flour mix
- 1–1/4 c granulated sugar
- 1/2 c cocoa
- 1t baking soda
- 3/4 t salt
- 1/4 t baking powder
- 3/4 t Ener G® xanthan gum

Liquid:

- 1–1/2 eggs (visually approximate)
- 1/2 c extra light olive oil
- 3/4 t vanilla
- 1c warm water

Follow the mixing and beating instructions for chocolate cake for the smaller pan.

For the 9–1/2 x 5–1/2 pan, bake at 350° for 43–44 minutes.

For the 9-inch round pan, bake at 350° for 37–40 minutes.

The cake is done when a toothpick inserted in the middle comes out clean. Cool completely and remove the cake from the pan for easy slicing.

FROSTINGS

If you want that homemade touch or want to know exactly what ingredients are in your frostings, these recipes are great choices. The buttery flavor is superb!

Vanilla Frosting

The amount below will be enough for the 8–1/2 x 4–1/2 pan. If you prefer a lot of frosting, simply double the recipe.

 1–1/2 c powdered sugar
 1/4 c butter (Use Crisco® shortening if you don't want to refrigerate the frosting.)
 1/2 t vanilla
 2t water
 1t Ener G® Egg Replacer™ mixed with 2t additional warm water

Beat the powdered sugar, butter (or Crisco® shortening), vanilla, and water.

Add the Ener G® Egg Replacer™ mixed with the additional water and beat for 2 minutes.

Chocolate Frosting

Mix in 1T cocoa with the powdered sugar, increase the water to 3–1/4 t and proceed as above. The amount of Ener G® Egg Replacer™ with warm water is the same.

SWEET BREADS

Sweet breads are very versatile since you can serve them for breakfast or use as side dishes at other meals. Both the banana bread and corn bread are moist and winners with the family.

Banana Bread

Use an 8–1/2 x 4–1/2 pan.

Dry:

  1–1/4 c flour mix
  1/2 t baking soda
  1/2 t salt
  1/2 t Ener G® xanthan gum
  1T buttermilk powder *(Saco® brand)*
  5/8 c granulated sugar *(1/2 c + 2T)*

Liquid:

  3T extra light olive oil
  1 egg
  3/4 c mashed bananas *(1–1/2 to 2 bananas)*
  1/4 c warm water
  1/2 t vanilla

Preheat the oven to 350°.

Warm the egg in very warm water.

Shake the dry ingredients, except the sugar, in a closed container and set aside.

Mix the sugar and extra light olive oil in the mixing bowl and then blend in the egg.

Add the bananas, water, and vanilla, and beat until smooth. Stir in the mixed dry ingredients, pour into the lightly sprayed pan and bake for 40–45 minutes on the center rack. (Check at 40 minutes.) The bread is done when a toothpick inserted in the middle comes out clean. Cool completely and remove the bread from the pan for easy slicing.

Cornbread

Use a 9-inch pie pan.

Dry:

- 1/2 c + 2T flour mix
- 1/2 c cornmeal *(Corn flour may be used, but cornmeal is the best choice.)*
- 1/2 c granulated sugar
- 2t baking powder
- 1/2 t salt
- 1/2 t Ener G® xanthan gum

Liquid:

- 1 egg
- 1/4 c extra light olive oil
- 1/2 t vanilla
- 1/2 c 2% milk warmed for 40 seconds on medium in the microwave

Preheat the oven to 350° and warm the egg in very warm water.

Shake the dry ingredients in a closed container and set aside.

Beat the egg in the mixing bowl.

Add the oil and vanilla. Don't beat these.

Add the mixed dry ingredients and then the milk.

Blend these, and then beat for 3 minutes.

Pour the batter into a 9-inch pie pan lightly sprayed with vegetable spray and bake for 25 minutes.

Cover loosely with aluminum foil and bake for 5 more minutes (30 minutes in total).

PANCAKES AND WAFFLES

You can enjoy your weekend breakfasts again with this recipe that works for pancakes and also turns out great waffles in an Oster® Belgian waffle maker. There is no dripping and no mess!

Dry:

1c flour mix
2T + 1/2 t granulated sugar
2–1/8 t baking powder
1/2 t salt
1/8 t Ener G® xanthan gum

Liquid:

1 egg
2T corn oil
1/2 t vanilla
1/2 c 2% milk

Warm the egg in very warm water.

Warm the milk for 40 seconds on medium in the microwave.

Shake the dry ingredients in a closed container and set aside.

Beat the egg in the mixing bowl.

Add the oil and vanilla. Don't beat these.

Add the mixed dry ingredients and then the milk.

Blend these, and then beat for 3 minutes.

Tip: Pour the mixture into a pitcher for easy pouring.

Heat the lightly oiled frying pan on medium heat. Pour the batter and turn the pancakes when they bubble. Cook for about a minute longer. Take a peek underneath to see if the pancake is browned to your liking.

For waffles, follow your waffle maker baking instructions, but be very vigilant of the time.

This recipe will make about ten 4-inch pancakes or two Belgian waffles.

Tip: Light corn syrup makes a great syrup! You can also call the manufacturer of your favorite pancake syrup to see if it is gluten-free. Flavorganics® has a line of syrups without high fructose corn syrup.

Variation: Use extra light olive oil in place of the corn oil, and if possible, don't oil the nonstick pan or waffle iron. The result is a very light tasting pancake or waffle!

COOKIES

Sorghum flour and Ener G® Egg Replacer™, in addition to the regular egg, help gluten-free cookies tremendously! If you don't use sorghum flour, the cookies will still taste great, but they will not be as appealing visually.

You can make larger batches by doubling amounts. Classic chocolate chip cookies and bars are sure to please family and friends at any gathering, and the cinnamon sugar cookies are another top choice for those who love their cinnamon.

Chocolate Chip Cookies

Ingredients:

1–1/8 c flour mix
2t sorghum flour
1/2 t baking soda
1/2 t salt
1/2 t Bob's Red Mill® xanthan gum
1/2 c Crisco® shortening or butter
1/3 c granulated sugar
1/3 c brown sugar
1c chocolate chips

1 egg
1/2 t vanilla

Preheat the oven to 375° and warm the egg in very warm water.

Mix the sugars together and set aside; mix the dry ingredients (minus the chips) and set aside.

Combine the Crisco® shortening or butter, sugars, and vanilla. Beat until they are creamy.

Beat in the egg, and gradually add the mixed dry ingredients. Stir in the chips.

Drop teaspoonfuls of the batter onto a very lightly sprayed cookie sheet. Bake for 10–11 minutes. This recipe will make about 2 dozen cookies.

Let the cookies cool for 3 minutes on the cookie sheet, and then they are easier to remove for full cooling on a cooling rack.

For a *softer* chocolate chip cookie, use butter instead of Crisco® shortening, and beat in a mixture of 1t Ener G® Egg Replacer™ with 2t warm water after you cream the butter and sugar.

For the *8x8 pan*, spread the batter in the pan, lightly sprayed with vegetable no-stick cooking spray. If you are using Crisco® shortening, bake at 375° for 24 minutes. If you are using butter, bake for 28 minutes. If you are using mini chocolate chips, use 2/3 cup chips.

For a 9x13 pan, double the recipe and bake for 30–33 minutes at 375°.

Butter Cookies

Ingredients:

1–1/4 c flour mix
2 t sorghum flour
1/2 t baking powder
1/4 t salt
1/2 t Bob's Red Mill® xanthan gum
1 t EnerG® EggReplacer™with 2t warm water

1/2 c butter
1/2 c granulated sugar
1/2 t vanilla

Preheat the oven to 325°.

Shake the dry ingredients except the Ener G® Egg Replacer™ in a closed container and set aside.

Soften the butter and add the sugar gradually, beating until light and fluffy. Stir in the vanilla.

Mix the Ener G® Egg Replacer™ with the water in a separate small cup, add to the creamed butter and sugar, and beat for a minute.

Mix in the dry ingredients and shape into balls about an inch in diameter. Roll the ball in sugar or just rub the top of the ball in a mixture of 1/4 c sugar that was colored with a drop of red or green food coloring.

Place the balls on a very lightly sprayed cookie sheet and bake for 15 minutes. Let the cookies cool for 3 minutes on the cookie sheet, and then they are easier to remove for full cooling on a cooling rack. This recipe will make 18 cookies.

Mexican Wedding Cakes

Ingredients:

1–1/8 c flour mix
2t sorghum flour
1/2 t baking powder
1/2 t Bob's Red Mill® xanthan gum
1t EnerG®EggReplacer™ with 2t warm water
1/2 c chopped walnuts

1/2 c butter
2T confectioners powdered sugar
1t vanilla

Preheat the oven to 300°.

Shake the flours, baking powder, and xanthan gum in a closed container and set aside.

Soften the butter and add the powdered sugar gradually, beating until well blended. Stir in the vanilla.

Mix the Ener G® Egg Replacer™ with the water in a separate small cup, add to the creamed butter and sugar, and beat for a minute.

Mix in the dry ingredients, little by little. Add the nuts and mix well.

Shape into balls about an inch in diameter and place them on a very lightly sprayed cookie sheet.

Bake for 25 minutes, remove from the oven, and let the cookies sit for a minute. They are fragile.

Then dust them with confectioners sugar. Put powdered sugar into a bowl, and gently place the cookie in the sugar. Then take a spoonful of powdered sugar to sprinkle the top of the cookie. This recipe will make about 16 cookies. You can cool them on a piece of waxed paper or parchment paper laid on a cooling rack for less mess.

Cinnamon Sugar Cookies

Ingredients:

1–1/2 c flour mix

1T sorghum flour

1t cream of tartar

1/2 t baking soda

1/8 t salt

3/4 t Bob's Red Mill® xanthan gum

3/4 c granulated sugar

1/4 c butter

1/4 c Crisco® shortening

1 egg warmed in very warm water

Cinnamon mixture: 1/4 c sugar + 2t ground cinnamon

Preheat the oven to 400°.

Shake the dry ingredients (except the sugar) in a closed container and set aside.

Beat the 3/4 c sugar, the butter, shortening, and the egg in the mixing bowl.

Stir in the mixed dry ingredients.

Shape the dough into balls a little over an inch in diameter. Roll the balls in the cinnamon mixture and place them on a very lightly sprayed cookie sheet.

Bake for 9 minutes. Let the cookies cool for 3 minutes on the cookie sheet, and then they are easier to remove for full cooling on a cooling rack. This recipe makes about 2 dozen cookies.

BROWNIES

These chocolate brownies will definitely satisfy your chocolate cravings. The Rich Brownies are slightly cake-like and rich in taste, and the Richer Brownies have the traditional thick, chewy texture. No one will ever know they are gluten-free!

Rich Brownies

Use an 8 x 8 pan.

Ingredients:

3/4 c flour mix
1/2 t Ener G® xanthan gum
1c granulated sugar

2 oz chocolate (Use 6T cocoa + 2T oil)
2 eggs warmed in very warm water
1/2 c butter
1t vanilla

Preheat the oven to 350°.

Shake the flour mix and xanthan gum in a closed container and set aside.

Mix the cocoa and oil (extra light olive oil) in a separate bowl and set aside.

Cream the butter and sugar and then add the cocoa and oil mixture.

Beat the eggs in one at a time.

Add the vanilla and then the flour mix with xanthan gum until well-blended only.

Pour the batter into the lightly sprayed pan and bake for 30 minutes.

Variation: For an even more cake-like brownie, add 1t baking powder and 1/4 t salt to the flour mix. Both brownie types are a little bit fragile, but they taste great! Bake at 350° for 30 minutes.

Richer Brownies

Use a 9 x 9 pan.

Ingredients:

3/4 c flour mix	1/4 c extra light olive oil
1/4 t baking soda	3/4 c granulated sugar
1/4 t salt	2T water
1/2 t Ener G® xanthan gum	1t vanilla
2c chocolate chips	2 eggs

Preheat the oven to 325°.

Shake the flour mix, baking soda, salt, and xanthan gum in a closed container and set aside.

Warm the eggs in very warm water.

Heat the extra light olive oil, sugar, and water together until the mixture starts to bubble, and then remove the pan or bowl from the heat source.

Add 1 cup chips and the vanilla, and stir the mixture until the chips are fully melted. Then place this mixture into a mixing bowl.

Beat in the eggs, one at a time.

Blend in the mixed dry ingredients.

Stir in the rest of the chips (1 cup). Place the batter into a 9-inch or 9–1/2-inch square baking pan very lightly sprayed with vegetable spray and spread with a spatula.

Bake at 325° for 25–27 minutes. An 8-inch square pan requires 40–44 minutes.

SHORTBREAD

Plain or topped with jelly or jam, use this shortbread as a substitute for pastries. Enjoy as a breakfast treat or dessert with your favorite beverage.

Use an 8 x 8 pan.

Ingredients:

1c flour mix
1t sorghum flour
1/3 c powdered sugar
1/2 t Bob's Red Mill® xanthan gum
1/2 t baking powder
1/4 t salt

1 egg
3/8 t vanilla *(1/4 t + 1/8 t)*
3-1/2 T butter flavored Crisco® shortening
Crisco® sticks have convenient tablespoon
    markings.

Preheat the oven to 350°.

Shake the dry ingredients in a closed container and set aside.

Warm the egg in very warm water.

Beat the egg with a hand mixer.

Add the vanilla, the mixed dry ingredients, and the Crisco® butter-flavored shortening. Use a spatula to mix it into a rather stiff batter.

Place the batter into the lightly sprayed pan and spread with the spatula. Bake at 350° for 25 minutes. Cool the pan on a cooling rack. Frost the shortbread if desired.

If you are using Ener G® Egg Replacer™ instead of the egg, double the shortening to 7T and the powdered sugar to 2/3 c. Baking time is the same.

PIE CRUST

In the summertime, at Thanksgiving time, or any time, it's nice to savor a scrumptious slice of pie. Single crust pies are easier to handle than double crust pies, but either way, the outcome is delectable!

This will make two crusts for one 9-inch pie.

Ingredients:

2c flour mix
2t sorghum flour
1/4 t baking powder *(scant 1/4 t)*
1t salt
1t Bob's Red Mill® xanthan gum
1T + 1t granulated sugar

1-1/3 eggs beaten *(visually approximate the 1/3 egg or measure 11 cc egg white and 4 cc yolk. Use a child's medicine dispenser to measure.)*
1T + 1t water
1/8 t vanilla
2t apple cider vinegar
13 T Crisco® shortening *(3/4 c + 1T) (It can be half butter flavored Crisco® shortening and half regular Crisco® shortening)*
Crisco® sticks have convenient tablespoon markings.

Combine the dry ingredients and shake in a container with a lid. Place this in a mixing bowl and cut in the Crisco® shortening with a fork.

Combine the liquid ingredients.

Mix everything together, shape it into a ball, and chill this for an hour. The dough will be easier to work with when it is chilled.

Divide the ball into 2 parts; the bottom crust needs to be slightly larger than the top crust.

Roll the crusts between slightly floured (gluten-free floured) pieces of plastic wrap. Carefully place the bottom crust into the pie plate.

Put in your favorite pie filling (one or two cans according to taste) and carefully place the top crust on. It's fragile, but be patient; it will work out. Flute the edges if you'd like, and pierce the top with several slits. Put foil around the edges and bake according to the pie filling instructions.

Tips: Add 1t cinnamon to the canned apple pie filling. If desired, you can also add 2T butter, cut in pieces, on top of the canned apple or cherry pie filling.

Place a cookie sheet underneath the pie plate when baking.

To bake a pie shell, place the crust in the pan, poke with a fork in several places, and bake at 425° for 10 minutes. (This recipe will make two pie shells.)

Pecan pie works very well with one crust. Follow the instructions on the Light Corn Syrup bottle purchased from the supermarket. Make two pecan pies with this recipe or freeze one crust for later use or divide the ingredients in half and make one pie crust.

CONCLUDING ENCOURAGEMENT

I wish you all the best as you embark and journey with your gluten-free baking! With these recipes, you have the tools to prepare and enjoy the same kinds of breads and baked goods that you ate prior to your diagnosis. You can satisfy your cravings and know that you are not missing out on your favorites. Adapting to celiac disease does become second nature to you, and you can go about your daily routines without worrying about mealtimes. If you live with celiac disease, going gluten-free is the only way to a healthier you!

—Mary Brown

INDEX